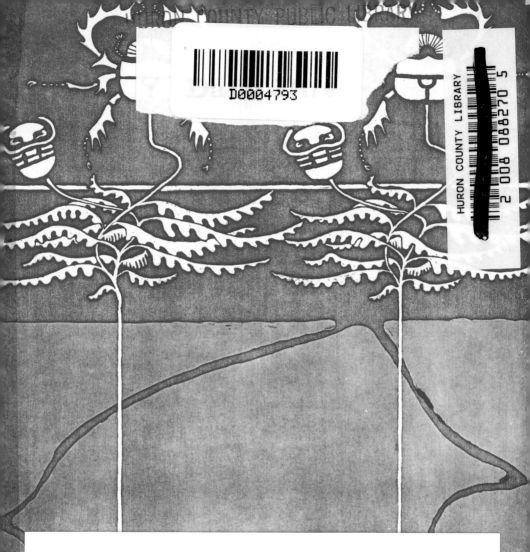

ALTER SUBLIME

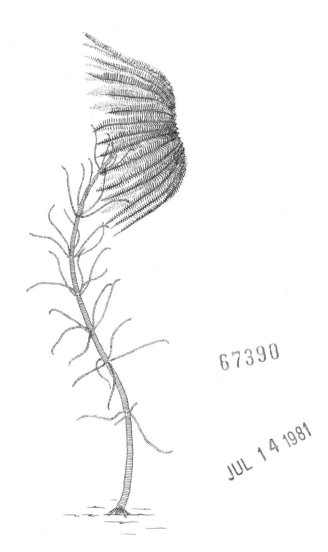

CHRISTOPHER DEWDNEY

THE COACH HOUSE PRESS · TORONTO

This book was written between Fall 1974 and Fall 1979
(excluding the lost poems from *Fovea Centralis*).

Some of these poems have occurred in *The Capilano Review,*
Brick, A Hundred Posters, Periodics, Only Paper Today,
Grosseteste Review, This, Bezoar/Winter, The Tamarack Review,
L=A=N=G=U=A=G=E and *CBC Radio.*

Published with the assistance of the Canada Council
and the Ontario Arts Council.

ISBN 0-88910-208-2

This book is dedicated to the memory of
my father, Selwyn Dewdney.

Contents

ALTER SUBLIME

Alter Sublime

Between the shadow
and the reflection between
(between) the shadow
and our eyes
                    lies.
the virtual image.
Once opened a crack
and the stars came pouring through.

Hovering over the febrile narcissus
of your after-image
the Word surfaces in cruel cisterns.
Our memory seizures expended
in the last ripples of
                    the virtual shadow.
As if perspective
cutting along the lines of focus
were progressively less & less adroit
in the articulation of creation.
A bloodless coup
in the military junta of the Vampire. It

It is this miraculous fire
which he has made for himself.
A glowing mantle
the device of ice-crystals
to inscribe the pool's clear fascination.
Do you know him?
The image falls crashing to his feet
again and again.
Each time a world reduced
to smooth glowing shards.
                    (pause, reset)

Divine anaesthesia
correct everlasting.

It is the, it is
like a hole
that runs through everything.
Seen
it is altered.
Grasped
it is broken.
Strange herald,
predator of the adoration,
it is the mind
eating itself.

The column unspeakable

Turn your radio to the microwave bands and listen there.

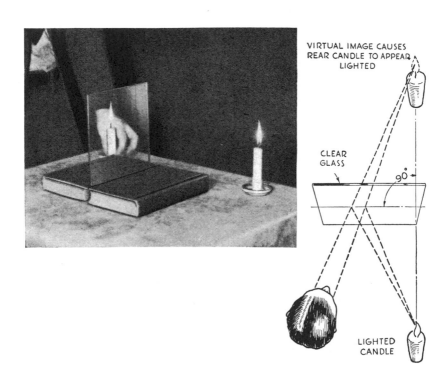

VIRTUAL IMAGE CAUSES
REAR CANDLE TO APPEAR
LIGHTED

CLEAR
GLASS

90°

LIGHTED
CANDLE

It is a cold winter night. A waning moon is rising over the desolate fields, articulating the occasional woodlot. You feel warm and rested as though you had just disembarked from a vehicle. You (you) turn around to look for one but you are alone. You have walked out here during an attack of amnesia & have only now awakened to your plight. The night is deep & incredibly cold. The stars fire like ancient insects, dazzling through a coal seam.

It is a warm spring night. A new moon is just setting above the glow of the sunset. You are walking home on a path through the woods. The leaves have just begun to open. You hear an owl hooting in a clear tiny voice that seems to emanate from within your head. You look up to see the owl. It is sitting on a long slender branch directly over the path. The owl is not a real owl but the caricature of an owl like a cartoon. It disappears. You are on your knees in the path sobbing and laughing. When it disappeared you lost your soul momentarily.

You are a child. You are standing on the prow of an old wooden boat in the centre of a muddy tropical river. Your mother is stroking your hair. You turn and look behind you are not alone. You are lying on a bed in a cabin. He is an old East Indian, he smiled, his muscles rippling with the smooth sinuous movement of the solitary oar. Outside the trees are humming in the starlight. The forest on the riverbank dissolves into a powdery retinal light. Your eyes are closed. You are outside looking down on the cabin & forest at the same time as you are lying in bed. The old man had turned into a cobra that is now rearing its gaping mouth just behind your head, nerves creaming as magnetic funnel pulls you out the back of your head trailing nervous system the needle-teeth cool deep into your flesh.

Nothing must disturb the stillness of this perfect reflection.

You are standing in the British Museum looking at a bronze Hindu sculpture in small glass case. You are leaning over inspecting it closely. It is a small boat, intricately carved depicting a hooded cobra rising out of the helm of the boat and stretching forward with its open mouth just behind the head of a figure standing on the prow of the boat. The figure's hand rests on the point of the bow, which is actually the tip of the snake's tail.

It is a clear windy day. You are in a canoe in a lake it is a clear windy day in Northern Ontario. It is an August afternoon and you are in a canoe it has been clear and windy for several days. And there is a silence turning everything in on yourself. It is August and in the wind there is a silence. In the stillness of the shallow inlet there is a silence, there is a single bird, confidential. Its song unfamiliar & beautiful. The shallow inlet. It sings in a strangely staggered series of descending fifths, ending on a note so wise and fearful your heart races in the eerie perfection of it. In the silence of it.

I was thought walking towards you. I thought (were you saying something?) I was trying to prove something. I thought (I thought I was trying to save someone) I was trying to talk to you. (I was walking towards you) I thought (a lion was walking beside you) we could talk (trying to speak to you) to each other. I thought (you were speaking to shortchange yourself) I was trying to prove something. Trying (to spite) someone out. There.

Every muscle in your body is rigid. There is a thickness in the air of the room, like a silent scream latent in the heavy peripheral fog surrounding you are transfixed. You are staring through a mirror at the human trapped in the room behind the mirror. In the second you failed to recognize your own reflection you separated. The human in the other room crouches & begins to approach your opening, eyes wide with fear. You are only dimly aware of your own irresistible motion towards the opening. The mirror is no longer silvered. The thickness coalesces into a binary scream, both of you screaming sound bending the room as your foreheads plunge through each other's foreheads through each other's symmetry. The room breaking into flashing white shards of interstellar nothingness. The world reduced to smooth glowing shards.

It is a warm sunny morning in early May. The sun has been up for an hour though the streets & sidewalks are still wet from a heavy rain the night before. You are standing beside a low cobblestone wall skirting the base of a hill. You are standing in the middle of the sidewalk. You have stopped walking to stare at the wall. The sun shines just over the brow of the hill to your left, throwing the side of the wall facing you into a shade illuminated by the sky. You are trembling at once with the chill of early morning & the incredible revelation that is unfolding itself in the small colonies of thyme and moss growing on the wall. Each cell of every tiny leaf & flower has been crystallized with living jewels of infinite detail. Every grain a vision unearthly. Your body is hollow a joyous vapour in the form of a child. You look up to see the small city surrounding this hill, a large limestone building at its summit. You are 8 years old. It is a spring morning in the early 1950s. This is Sunnyside or perhaps Kitchener. You are beyond tears.

The previous night during the party he had been staring at the bamboo curtains. There had been no diminishment of immediacy since then. He awoke from a ten hour sleep as if he had just turned his head away from regarding them. As if he had just turned to make a point in a conversation with somebody who had inexplicably vanished. Not only was everyone long gone, but he was alone in his bedroom, clutching desperately at the rapidly fading and absurdly banal memory of the bamboo curtains.

Your life will become an act of faith secured by a single act of faithlessness....

There is a substance which, for simplicity's sake, I shall call Ice. This substance, clear and brittle in its natural state, can be molded into any form. Also, when dropped, it will emit the sound of whichever object it is molded into a likeness of. If it is shaped like a banana it will sound like a banana when it is dropped. Needless to say if it is shaped like a bird it will not sing, but it will emit a soft swish-thud if dropped upon the floor.

It is the mind eating itself.

There is (between the silence in words) a silence between the sounds, between the words. Like (it begins) a microphone so (fedback on itself) sensitive it begins to feedback on itself (it begins in the absence of sound) in the absence (sensation) of sound. (sensation)

A low (utterance) barely discernible hum begins within (beginning to make sense?) a minute of the last (utterance) spoken word. If (the feedback is interrupted) another sound occurs, in this case a soft (if) whisper (ed) into the ear of a particular (this means you) person, then the (interruption is feedback disappears) feedback is interrupted and the hum (and the hum) disappears.

Unapprehended the hum (will) mounts quickly (summer enclave) to a deafening crescendo.

During some conversations this sensitivity is greater and the feedback process will begin quite early after a pause, sometimes within an matter of seconds, making a pregnant silence caesarean with lingual foetuses.

Using a tool to alter another tool is the beginning of artificial intelligence.

Before remora chemitrodes (calling Dr. Delgado) consciousness was a function of the brain, now the brain (calling Dr. Delgado) is a function of consciousness.

(one word spoken softly)
Espionage selecting random elements from the real & transmuting
them into hierophantic analogies of the highest order.
Charmed particles in the cloud chamber.

Silos are parachutes
with a reinforced concrete flight-plan.

Poem using lines spoken by Suzanne

What you feel as your body
is only a dream. The mind also
is a slave. You are asleep.
You are asleep, what you feel
as your mind is only a dream. The
dream also, is only a slave.
You are a dream, what you feel
as your slave is only a mind.
The body also is a mind. You
are asleep
in the gentle theft of time. (time)

Anecessity

There is no oral tradition.
There is amoral tradition.
Instinct. A sense
of concentric liqueurs
mutually arriving at their
respective levels.
That's a moral. A thorn
breaking off just under the skin.
Barbs relying on
your movement
to work their way in.

Byron Bog

A man wishes to be
what he means to himself.
By whatever means
for his self. Self
contests an equivocal battle
which logic
is not natural. I
thought there was something
out there.
(too articulate)
I lived a lie until it became
the truth. Articulation.
There was something out. (there) Article
of speech.

What you see is
what you get.
I am thinking
despite myself.
I feel pleasant strangeness
when I meet you.
I thought I was trying
to prove something.
I thought you said
you were thinking
to spite yourself.

Radio Symmetry

At everything we see
occipital a reconstruction retinal.
Mind imparting a clarity
unoptical. I was shown
insensate islands in the poems.

'Seeing as is.' they believing say.
It's on the record.
                    Everything
you say will be used against you.
You have the right to remain silent
while retaining a witness.
You have the right
to solicit the stabilizer.

A warning frightful,
weathered grey signboard in limestorm wind.
This times the dream was even.
Mind's known factors assembled together
small & huddled in the corner
of the enlarging room.
The held image mutates in memory,
in hands like clumps of wet sand
drying
sliding out in the hot sun.

These time the dream
is on you.

United

I would walk through the hissing January blizzard.
I would walk through the shimmering mirage
                                        of gas flames
like a flickering blue moss, glowing
beneath my feet.
I would walk down the long hospital corridor
to where you lay.
I would come down small boats in the tiny
tributaries of your national river system.
I would pray to incantations of your wholeness,
your divinity.
I would wait centuries to hold you,
carve through aeons of rock to gaze
at last upon your fossil.
I am demented and the cold & empty nights are
unbearable. I gnaw on the poison
that distills these words. I am ravaged
in the thin plane of the blizzard
just above the horizon.
I am surrounded by unendurable beauty
endless a succession of this truth.
Manifold destiny. May the cradle of the ocean
spawn our likeness in years to come.

Boreal Electric

For my lady, keeper of my wound.
GRAFFITI

She is the twilight intangible, a thin instruction
burning within the envelope generators. Alter
sublime in the cenozoic asylum. And
I am case-hardened. Natty causal an
auto-facsimile. Denoting cold fire.
There is nothing sentimental
about these rocks. I am
the envelope generator growling
in the shifting code facsimiles of night.

Zone trances. Indigo.

I would have her mouth the words
'statutory rape' slowly. Arrested
for intent to denote this line.
This lodestar being visible only
to the discerning eye.

The disconcerting eye.

Dreadlocks at the Helm

for Lise

Still ciphers hanging in the air. Light cord
cobras animated with tradewinds
poised suspended to strike
                                  above
the perfect flesh of a woman
sleeping.
These her guardians averted
by a promise. Making us linger here
in the sweet darkness which is night.
She dawns on us, hung over like an eclipse
of recognition.

British lagoons unfurling
our sins in absentia & light years
the legions we left behind.

This our communion fantastic with
                                  palms
a series of still explosions disturbing
the white crescent of the beach.
Our eyes mineralized in the moonlight.
In our ears
the daemonic cacophony of night beasts.

Fruit bat at the mango.
Fruit bat at the papaya.

Dreadlocks at the helm.

½ second

Path of the fruit bats
eating a papaya
from the papaya tree.

Brain Pan

I am beside myself.
I am sitting beside myself
believing myself & reeling you in
from an autonomous vista that
has no replica.
Reduplication is meaningless
in this contexts.
I am out of context, by the text
it was a textbook case
& case-hardened abounding delight
in every sense
the arousing thunder.
The valley & the gate,
I am the Dundas. I am the beside myself
to tell you something & even this
is out of context. A line
with no automatic lures. Ha.
I am the guileless night intruder
with no jokes to whisper hoarsely
in your ear. Tragedy has burned me
clear. I see a hole in your head
you could shine a CN diesel-light through.

There are no jokes in the train-tunnel.
No furtive-eyed creatures breathlessly awaiting
the passing of the next train.
The trains here follow no schedule
there are no engineers, brakemen or
passengers. Only the lovers, who seldom
whisper at all. There are no recording
instruments & strychnine rat-parties
for visiting celebrities. Only the

hoarse whispering of grass & the
crackle of fires started by sparks
from the train wheels.
This is crucial in the cycle
this is critical in the process
of becoming that which we are.
Undefatigable delight in persisting
at directing our own extraction.

She smiled through the tears.
One ray of sun down on the broken glass floor
of the cool jungle. We are
what we thought we were, but didn't
have the time to decide before
we made up our minds. There are no decisions.
I think in film clips.
Who has time for movies?
You didn't really think
that you could cry &
then laugh & then cry
so quickly did you? Time
makes us liars. I wanted to
be true in time. Ha, what did
I know. An infatuation with
deceit would lead me to the truth.
The *same* deep glassy eyes that
my vision keeps referring to,
like a specialist in search of a generality.
If you know the desert, signal
for I am one of you. I have
seen the sliver of a new moon
in the full blaze of a desert afternoon.
I have heard thousands of telephone conversations
humming in the wires during desert storms. Lovers

straining to hear each other through the
long distance static.
'Is that you? Are you there?'
In the jungle there is a species
of small beetle that eats down
through the copper core of the telephone wires.
Sometimes miles of wire are destroyed
in this manner. In the jungle no
strain-sparks set off grass fires. The
glass floor heaves under the vision
of our arbitrators.
The arbitrators have no sense of humour.
They merely measure out our proportions
of pain & gladness, as one would
loose sand through the fingers
or strike a flint to start a locomotive.

The initiative escapes us
because the real inertia is not downhill.
It is in the finality of this vision
that the wires speak
& all the peoples of the tunnel unite.
In a single track mind, burning
with its head-lamp buried in your eyes,
in your thighs.

It is an early May night in Hamilton.
It is raining.

Remora

Certain parasites rather
like mediums for exchange
attach themselves
to those things which we desire.
The exchange of dry goods.
We are causal archaeologists
seeking an explanation for the rise
of our ontogenetic civilization.
The apple frequently
returns to its beholder.
What once bitten
the apple does not ascribe to
is an oracle.
Had one bitten elsewhere,
off of a hunk largely
bitten of divisible pieces of itself,
perhaps we could have limited
the activities of the reclamation men.

Little meaning
is attached to these phrases.
It is almost as to say if
one were not diminished
in the way a bitten apple diminishes
piece by moon-like crater piece.
As if the train
halted in iiiiii's.
The zzzzzzzed of your being there.

Sleeping is as easy
as sawing off a log.
We wake up wen

the lawg hits us. Hipgnosis.
One becomes small
as if in a tiny aquarium.
How much detail
can be confided in one place?
'The restoration is proceeding well
except, of course, for the finer details.'
Or that what we had, at best,
calmly accepted was venerable mistake.
The apple lands with a thud
on the sleeper's head.
He awakes & immediately thinks
'Gravity!'

But these are glimmerings
between the strokes
between the spokes
of Her pouring through.
Her voluminous heady rushing of waters.
And the stranger's laugh rings through the canyon.
While in the rapids the
apples jostle with logs.
Will is apparent even whirling
dervish will is particularly
this detail.

Poem

for Calla

The child feels awesome electro-magnetic symphonies
her soul a pitiless receiver. She understands flowers are
what they do & that a flower opening is
an act of faith
as she is an act of
profound faith.

Profound sleep of the faithless while
the hydro-electric generators
crackle & gape in the March starlight.
Her pitiless electric beauty.

Think Pool

Log; May 31st
    1. Spent day in bars recording the conversation of drunks.
    2. Replayed conversations using two actors to reproduce script at normal interaction speed.
    3. Picked out aberrant logic constructs in a 'regular setting' scan.
    4. Deducted linguistic pattern analogizing the pathology.

Listening (sit-com) was graded (radio network) for them (calculating) by (a kind of) yellow journalism. They wanted a (helio) concentric model (no ledger buffs) (hedonistic amulets) (rat patrol). I couldn't see the force (d) field for the press. They would (obviously) graze until the top-soil (pleated in kindness) was razed.
    a) Indicated as a specialty in rear mountwork?
    b) This rendition would have done better in a hotel room. ('You could hardly tell them apart sir.')

Objects (are electrons moving fast enough to) occupy solid space. (Can be witnessed than in less an half hour.) A contact (gregorian subvagina) would have caused (Mah Jong) a regular set of autonomous novae. (We.) Could hardly be expected (no assembly required) to discern the progression (especially) at this speed.

There are words that are standing waves between the words. Interference nodes virtually stationary in the regular emission of morphotactics. There are poems that are the standing waves between real poems. Standing waves fabricated by words vibrating within the resonance memory gives them.
    Standing waves.

A series of (consecutively finer and finer) realizations (rampant antennae) came here (upward mobility in the feeding frenzy) forward. To be human (stepping razor) is to have done it all over again. (Lest the credits fail to mention her.)

From this vantage the resistance dwindles to a trickle, the occasional burst of static over the short-wave. The short-wave. Pause. Reset. Edonilap (retro-active) in the palindrome of figurative evolution. O! your would rent a truck? You have the right to remain silent while retaining a witness. You have the right to solicit the stabilizer.

He sat down at the control panel and switched subject mode from Miscellaneous to Love. He turned the automatic editor to Black Mountain and pressed run.

He pushed the short term (forget) button and then switched to scan. In this way the image lag wouldn't make the machine prefer its own creation.

There is a song (telephone in the deep end of the pool) that recalls (I think it is for you) certain memories (at the bottom), but they were stolen (not by me). The clouds (didn't come that night) & meteors. (one skipped)

Specialize in evoking the transition zones in someone's emotionality. Those ambiguous moments between emotions, between thought and action, when a person is in the process of switching personae. Your conversation will become a series of planned statements that are constructed to elicit this specific response. The statement is not real in that *you* are saying something, but rather you say that which will alter the emotional status of the person you're talking to. Baited declarations leading in directions *not always* controllable.

Log; June 1st.

Those who couldn't appeal the restraints bound them to their word.

Exploding Hearts

'I've heard a heart go,' he said. 'Sounded like the sound my mom made when she ripped apart the ribcage of a chicken under a wet towel.'

The heart tears itself apart with the power of its own muscles. They say the blood pressure obtained while the heart is in its last two beats is incredible.

Everything is suddenly red.

The blood shoots out of the eyes like a horned toad. Accurate up to 20 metres.

Control Data

The subject, a continuity consultant in his late fifties, exhibited inordinate fear of commonplace objects and complained of spastic hair-trigger orgasms. After two hours of consultation we recommended a four month term in Hamilton. Sentence to be served consecutively.

★

Human beings are a catalyst freeing information into the cosmos in the same manner that plants free oxygen into the atmosphere, unknowingly perpetuating higher forms of intelligence.

★

There were a group of protesters with the words 'the words written across their T-shirts' written across their T-shirts.

Sunspots

The dominant individual is the one most out of control.

★

'You don't seem to understand officer. You see 'amorality' is a belief that precludes me from any legal proceedings.'

Vigilance

I am a sensualist, attenuated by constant vigilance.

★

Music adds an unnatural glory to our lives.

★

Language was given to us by aliens, as a tool.

★

Only the adjectives have been changed to protect the names of the innocent.

★

If I were in your shoes you'd be wearing size nine.

★

The future is simply amnesia in reverse.

Lion Annihilate Himalaya

The 'saviour' always takes the fall.

★

I've got a soft spot for psychopaths.

★

Your parents never told you this but the doctor who delivered you tried to strangle you at birth.

★

Babies are externalized genitals. (hence the comparison)

★

Humiliation of the illuminatii.

★

A paper entitled 'The successful reversal of satori in zen monks using surgical intervention.'

Surface Error

I was told of a horizon contained in a single point. The parabola is a cylinder of unlimited wealth & power within the numeric possibilities of the cosmos. As we know affixed atop a high stone tower at the centre of the reflecting surface. There are most likely 200 billion 'earths' like the landscape visible from our own in this universe. The Radio Telescope a mistake or some annoying detail. This is about as many is a parabola. Radio a detachment of men as there are atoms in a raindrop. Many of these earths are controlled from the Ariel cabin. Listen to the electromagnetic emanations from the cosmos. The only difference in an otherwise perfectly offending tree, rock, stream or house. Parallel planet would be that castle to remove. To do this they ceaselessly scan the heavens, in 1892. On this other 'earth' the repository for the Point* would have landed on a whorf in France. A centimetre which cannot be conceived in space/ time as we articulated the Horizon Garden of singularity. Know it eventually the identical whorf on our perfection. By reducing the visible landscape into a flaw in an otherwise perfectly synonymous earth in the distant depths of the universe.

This event would represent the only information derived from the telescope. In some copies radiates out of the Point. Certain people could not move from state of solipsistic error. If the Point variates even monstrous mutations would roam through city parks. The street you were turning onto would have immediately rendered the entire garden useless. Centrally fixed point wouldn't have been born. The Radio Telescope goes 'rampant'. A rampant antenna usually slave labour. Signals located a little distance to track mind. In others, ie humans or remote-control devices would also have involved the structural detriment of the installation. The already over-taxed village communities are usually destroyed. For this reason rampant antenna utilizing reverse matter cannot be constructed within a 400 kilometre radius of Kettle Point. The energy field surrounding the alternative in the outer shell, or memory jacket of the concretion.

These telekinetic disturbances arise out of the outer shell. A telekinetic surface error in the usual thermonuclear annihilation. Recent theoretical concretions might produce installations possible to construct an Anti-dish. Both the dish and the Antidish would eradicate each other. To believe that there is a rampant antenna between the memory jacket and the concretion is a lens of thin red oil. The concretion slowly expands at a pleasing equatorial. Grasping the parabloid by its peripheral material assimilates the surrounding limestone. The property of the cylindrical hub so that thousands of years. The master equatorial invested in a glass on a table. The azimuth cabin would, over a thousand years, create a large glass sphere. At this point fission in slow motion.

The lens of oil allows the concretion to roll smoothly.

Déjà vu

Reduplicative
Paramnesia

Installation

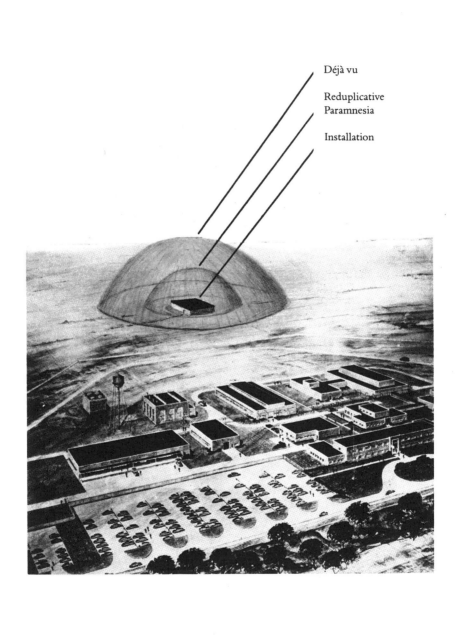

LOST POEMS
FROM
FOVEA CENTRALIS

Some Accidents

Richard bashed his face unfortunately.
And Tony received quite a nasty cut
half an inch below his eyebrow.
The cook took the cork-screw to
Melinda, who bled furiously but didn't
put out the sizzling fritters and battles.
Sally had her wrist crushed by an elevator.
Cliff caught a fist-sized rock in the eye.
Sue Ellen took two inches of broom-splinter
under her thumbnail.
Dave's toes were crushed by a rolling manhole cover.
Ann picked up a disc with razor sharp edges.

Density

There is a limit beyond which
density cannot function.
Density is a function of art.
As I walk down the street
a poem resounds faintly throughout
the landscape, a xerox fog
blurring the already tenuous
exploration of my perceptions.
Casually grimacing into a hand-grenade.
The bust you claim to represent
your present 'state of mind'
resembles most the udder abandonment
of cows in a pasture.

And why now, when your favourite
words are arranged with
meticulation beyond criticism
do you treacherously refuse
to acknowledge your own failure.

Poem

I have abandoned the field of swords & teeth
for an island, secure and remote.
From here you can see the machines
bumping quietly into each other at night.
I have abandoned the roses & absolute horror
for a church, secular and invoked.

Radar gets you by, that's why
monkey likes to stare fire in the eye.

Poem

And when I kissed you
the stars over the river flickered slightly
and were recorded. The design of the moon
through leaves, is to reduce a certain
inevitability into dance
and play with the odds, which
when stacked high enough
articulate gravity &
point in one steady finger
to the moonlight on one side of your face.

Haiku

My roof was once firm
yet now it cannot even
keep the stars out.

The Sensitive Recording Equipment

Now that you are tangible in
the sensitive recording equipment
I would like to point out a few things.
That direction you were headed in
is completely frugal, I had to give you a hand
if you realize, temporarily ... unless!

Souvenir

In each small vision of itself
by the waning gold of an August afternoon
a small ivory case with a gold trim
is opened to reveal the splendid photograph.

LOG ENTRIES

This Command

eased into gravitational on the dark side of the planet. For the mind is most at home in pure mind, which is emptiness. Its face still bore the traces of an ancient supernova. The signals were profuse but cryptic.

We had a good idea of what we would find before we got here. In the diversity of creation we had played favourites. The higher the evolution of a planet the more active its dark side. Night welcomes the starships out of love for its sister, deep space. The starships are genetically guided.

Already its artificial satellites flashed by us. Heretical paraphs of the surface technology. Crystals configured directly in the minds of these

Chlamydospores blowing in the solar wind.

For we seek the beginning of this command.
Ancient as the light
from distant stars.

equals the complexity of the vision. He is possessed either by rote or naturally of perceptual simultaneity & calibrates all the phenomena in any given situation. Thus in a room where music is playing on a phonograph he will be aware of each musician's individual nuances & stylistic references while also monitoring the exact source & cause of every phenomenon presented to his perceptions at the time. The tiny hiss from the kitchen indicating that a water-sprayer filled with hot water is now sucking in air through its nozzle as the water contracts within, each flicker and dimming of the lights is traced to its subsequent transformer and load factors on the whole power grid are determined from the variations of the sub-stations. A faint odour of

And at night the limousines creep out of their lairs.

I was then rendered deaf. He told me I had to construct the music utilizing a new instrument whose range & tone I'd never heard. Its insidiously orchestrated solos were in a number of locations within the symphony. I knew my deafness was essential, for if I could mentally reconstruct the symphony I too would hear the universal theme & from that point be incapable of constructing the orchestration. The musicians also

The (other side of) the other (way) side.
We had to construct a prison around us
surer
than any lie. (the other side of) way.

conjured by his rustling music into the pipes. He kept the undifferentiated tissue, the shaman spittle, in the horn, articulating its brutish & powerful beauty through the finger stops. The behaviour of the daemon imprisoned in his horn bent one to visualize a grey mass, undifferentiated beauty, like thick shaman's spittle, so radiant that it was by inverse perception a grey & irritable slug, forced to substantiate its divinity by performing small feats. As one would teach a unicorn to hop over piles of construction blocks. When

jetty

The artist drew a portrait of someone staring at him. If there are two people in the same room with the portrait both will observe that the portrait is staring at them (each, themselves). This is the virtual stare, a rainbow of solipsism stretched between all those who are encompassed within the illusion. The fixed eyes of the idol in the mandatory witnessing of its own two-dimensionality.

Between the shadow
and the reflection between
(between) the shadow
and our eyes
          lies
the virtual image.
Virtually what we had
(had) expected. Virtuous
blessing of the handfed
illusion.

could determine climate only by insect size. We only had enough time to collect two or three representative species, on which we ran a comparative program using an absolute or basal latitude. Determining coordinates from that data

An octopus lying on the ice at half-time.

you spot a tornado the tornado immediately becomes conscious of you & will begin to move towards you until you look away &
stop thinking or visualizing it in your mind. By altering the mental
image

Mammato anticipation.
The fascinated are unearthly.

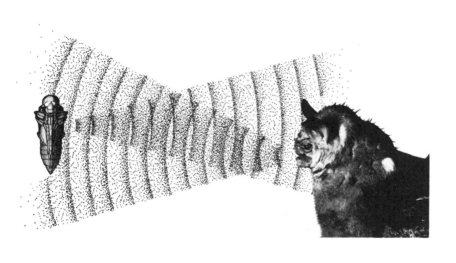

PARASITE MAINTENANCE

Introduction

Out of all the thoughts that present themselves to the poet's consciousness, there are certain 'special' sequences which he* chooses to record. Two conditions determine this choice: the first is editorial, i.e., the sequence's contextual relevance to his previous work & its concurrent modification (if any) by the 'critical milieu'; the second is a perception, a recognition if you like, of 'special status', due to the unique form of this linguistic invention which makes it differ from other inventions displayed to consciousness. Before choice, however, there obviously must be a process which generates these novel structures & presents them to consciousness. The following monograph is an examination of this process.

Homo sapiens & to a certain extent before him, Homo erectus, have engaged in several cumulative projects. Of necessity these projects were undertaken by the species, as their reification exceeded the normal life-span of an individual. The genetic engineering of domestic animals through selective hybridization is an example of such a cumulative project; language is another. Language, however, has in its turn had a much more profound effect on its creators than has the genetic engineering of domestic animals.

In the following monograph I propose that the evolution of language, inextricably bound with the evolution of our consciousness as a species[1], has diverged from its parallel & dependent status with the human species and has become 'animated', ie has, much like a model of artificial intelligence, or a robot, taken on a life of its own. Furthermore, I propose that special linguistic qualities peculiar to the English language, indicate the existence of a 'Governor' (in a mechanistic sense) with which the 'animated' language acts on the individual, restricting the limits of conceptualization.

Finally I also posit that the specialized use of linguistic inventions by the poet enables him to transcend the domain of the 'Governor', through the use of a special neural system singular to the ontogeny of the writer. This structure or system, a special condition of intelligence outside the realm of both the 'animated' language & the 'Governor', I refer to as the Parasite'.**

Two sections of this monograph, 'The House of the Living Language' and 'The Parasite', detail neurological functions in order to illuminate the physiology of the brain in the context of the proposed model. Parallel with the direction of the argument I have tried to provide a step-by-step layout of the basic neurology & neurochemistry necessary to orient the layman. The diagrams should be of some use in this process.

The important thing to realize in these models of localization is that even though the cortex of the brain (the grey matter) has specific areas which under electric stimulation activate memories, arm movements & so forth, the actual circuitry involved is remote from the point of electric stimulation & involves many sub-systems & loops. It's not as if the outside world is funnelled through a homunculus in the centre of the brain & then displayed on the neo-cortex in some kind of phrenological cinema. There are sub-stations & relays so profuse they confound the neuro-anatomists of today.

Remember always that there is no homunculus; 'I' is an illusion.

* The following article is more generally specific to the male brain. Recent findings by Jeannette McGlone (University Hosp., London, Ontario) indicate that language is organized somewhat differently in the brains of men and women.

** Because this process satisfies all the requirements for a parasitic symbiosis, if transposed into a biological analogy.

The Information Cylinder

The poet hosts a parasite.

The mechanistic relation of host and parasite is analogous to a parabolic antenna (radio telescope) and its focus. The focus is the parasite. The parabolic dish is the language cortex. The radio telescope becomes a model of the *bi-conscious* interface between 'the mind' and signals from the 'outside' which the poet receives. (Fig. 1)

The quality of mind in the radio telescope is its *will to select*.

FIGURE I: The Parabolic Antenna

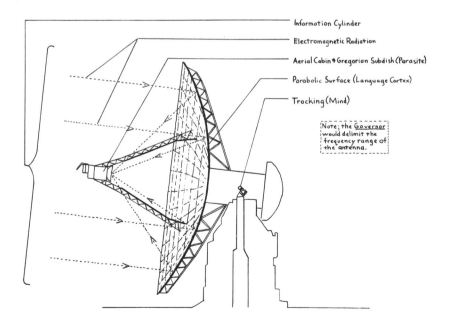

The medium into which these signals translate themselves is language, itself not only a complex and sublime tool, but also a living and evolving intelligence housing our most vital communotypes and is *itself not necessarily benevolent.* In fact the English language presupposes a special barrier, generally beyond perception, which precludes certain higher forms of conceptual reasoning from the age of verbal consciousness forward. This barrier is *the Governor,* and the success of the antenna to a large degree depends on the complex battle between *the Parasite* and *the Governor.* This contest is housed within the brain, and the spoils are those bits of information from beyond the limits of science and madness. This is privileged information. It places the poet in the same vanguard of research as physics, molecular chemistry and pure mathematics.

The theory of the 'outside', the details of which were pretty well worked out by Jack Spicer (a poet/ linguist who developed his theory of *seriality* and *dictation*[2] in San Francisco in the late fifties and early sixties), I take as *probatum est.* I will speak of *the Parasite* as an internal structure generating novel configurations. It is the *origin* of these signals that is outside. The *nature* of this origin is something I will not attempt to discuss here.

The Living Language

The word is composed of two parts, the kernel and the halo[3]. The kernel is the hard inner core of the word which exists taxonomically only, the halo is the aura of meanings, connotations and associations which surround the word. The term 'halo' corresponds to Whorf's term 'rapport'[4]. He believed rapport was a function of 'neural processes & linkages of the *non-motor* type, silent, invisible ...' The existence of the halo is easily demonstrable; simply repeating a given word over and over will drain the halo from it. The sound remaining, a pure taxonomic existence devoid of meaning, is the kernel. The halos of all words connect in one continuous field of energy to create the 'living language'. The living language exists in a symbiosis with the human 'host'.

As in other symbiotic relationships the organisms interface only where mutually beneficial, they are otherwise independent. The living languages have their own evolutionary autonomy and have, perhaps for the last fifty thousand years, been exerting a powerful influence on the course of human history. And this influence is most extreme on the English language users, for the operant disparity between language and host in the Indo-European languages attains its greatest distance in the synesthetic concept mutations of the English language. The following is a quote from Benjamin Lee Whorf, referring to exactly this quality of the English language.

> Synesthesia, or suggestion by certain receptions of characters belonging to another sense, as of light and colour by sounds and vice versa, should be made more conscious by a linguistic metaphorical system that refers to non-spatial experiences by terms for spatial ones.... It may be in this way our metaphorical language that is in some sense a confusion of thought is producing, through art, a result of far-reaching value — a deeper aesthetic sense leading toward a more direct apprehension of underlying unity behind the phenomena so variously reported by our sense channels.

The Word ('The word that made a man out of an ape and killed the ape in the process keeps man an animal the way we like to see him.' — William S. Burroughs[5].) is the most extreme manifestation of the living language, it is the Living Word, the signifier signified exponentially into the realm of pure being.

The Governor Indicated
(The Communolect & Dialectic Evolution)

In order to understand the workings of the Governor we must first examine other examples of the evolutionary autonomy & independence of the English language. (Remembering at all times that the language controls not just the way we think, but the way we *are*.) The two examples which most readily provide an insight into these mechanisms (in the order I shall be dealing with them), are the communolect and dialectic evolution.

The dialectic / communal metaphors, ie; 'Keep your eyes peeled.', henceforth referred to as the *communolect,* are weathervanes in the voice-wind of the living language. The voice of the living language as it can only be given voice, virtually belching through the oral sphincter of its host, of its body politic, and most certainly incontinent as it is vented by the very humans who substantiate its body. The communolect is the living language speaking in tongues. It says; 'You pulled a few strings & now you're in over your head. You're going to change your tune when you face the music.'

The communolect is governed by dialectic evolution, which determines its phrasing. The 'statement' of the communolect (see above) is always contemporary (synchronic) and sensitive to the broader sweeps of cogitation within the living language, though what we experience in the communolect is simply the interference pattern generated at the edge of an ocean of unfathomable cogitation.

Dialectic evolution is responsible for morphemic obsolescence, created by a language whose lexicon continues to evolve. (The written word is immobilized, a frozen moment in dialectic movement.) The Holy Grail legend, though having arrived fairly intact into our century, is nonetheless a case extant. At the time it was written the Grail Text was interpreted in two ways; firstly as a paragon of religious chivalry, secondly, as a symbolic text using alchemical mnemonic devices. Today our understanding of the Grail Myth is incomplete, many of the referentials & nuances of meaning are opaque to us. The synchronus communolect of the times, the connotative properties of the legend, are like the soft parts of a decaying fish, they rot away and leave only the skeleton to be preserved as a fossil. However, they do not really rot away in the sense that a real fish decays. Instead it is as if the fish's flesh was continuously re-assembled, fossilized particle by particle, morpheme-connotation by morpheme-connotation, over centuries of change in the living language; a living fossil whose flesh transubstantiates itself in the wind of dialectic modification. Therefore, because the words in some cases remain the same we are fooled into believing they mean the same thing. However, the interpretation changes at exactly the same rate as the interpreters change, making it an invisible process.

(In what ocean this 'fish' swims, or on what it feeds, is another question altogether.)

Occasionally there are regional occurrences of incredibly rapid dialectic evolution. English-speaking black communities, under specialized socio/ economic conditions in America, England, and most actively, Jamaica, are dramatically refiguring the English language. No single person changes the language. In an election rigged by the communolect, a dominant lingo is voted into office, there is no choice; the language is mutating by itself. The new Jamaican development, precipitated by a singular convergence of technology with the flowering of a true regional spirituality, is very distinct from the patois that preceded it. The Jamaicans are not only altering nouns and adjectival phrases, they are changing noun-phrases and verb tenses. They use the term 'I' to replace the terms 'me' and 'you'; 'you and I' or 'we' becomes 'I & I'. They also use 'I' as an easily substituted affix; 'vegetables' becomes 'I-tables', 'natural' becomes 'I-tal'. Also, their tense classifications are starting to become very hazy, obviously preparatory to a substantial shift in tense categories (and their parallel alterations of the language-user's experience of space/ time). For instance, one doesn't say 'I was last to arrive', one says 'I came here forward'.

Dialectic evolution in Jamaica is primarily configured by sympathetic magic.

Another ramification of the evolution of the communolect (as a factor of dialectic evolution) would be the evolution of the gestalt (as distinct from ancestral/ genetic archetypes). Freud was as correct for his time as Jung was for his. The psychic symbolism of the communal mind changes substantially within the space of a few years, indicating a much higher turnover rate than communolectic evolution.

Thus we see an immanent will shaping both the communolect and dialectic evolution. It is the inexorable structuring of these phenomena that indicates the powerful capabilities of the living language.

The existence of this independent intelligence, the living language, which sets up the Governor, has been hinted at by two outstanding linguists in this century; Benjamin Lee Whorf & Edward Sapir.

Human beings do not live in the objective world alone, nor alone in the world of social activity as ordinarily understood, but are very much at the mercy of the particular language which has become the medium for expression in their society. It is quite an illusion to imagine that one adjusts to reality essentially without the use of language and that language is merely an incidental means of solving specific problems of communication or reflection. The fact of the matter is that the 'real world' is to a large extent unconsciously built up on the language habits of the group ... We see and hear and otherwise experience very largely as we do because the language habits of our community predispose certain choices of interpretation.

EDWARD SAPIR

The phenomena of language are background phenomena, of which the talkers are unaware or, at the most, very dimly aware — as they are of motes of dust in the air of a room, though the linguistic phenomena govern the talkers more as gravitation than as dust would ... It is as if the personal mind, which selects words but is largely oblivious to pattern, were in the grip of a higher, far more intellectual mind which has very little notion of houses and beds and soup kettles, but can systematize and mathematize on a scale and scope that no mathematician of the schools ever remotely approached.

BENJAMIN LEE WHORF

In short the English language is a separate intelligence utilizing humans as the neural components in a vast and inconceivable sentience. The intact survival of this intelligence is threatened by one thing only, and that is the discovery and subsequent exploration of its plane of existence by ourselves, its human host. Safeguarding against this possibility is the function of the Governor. The Governor is an adamant limit beyond which, even in the loftiest flights of the intellect, it is impossible to conceptualize. And this limit, the Governor, operates in the most malignly subtle manner imaginable, as we have seen, by programming a conceptual limit into the very thought processes which fuel the flight of the intellect itself. Thus, not only is the limit adamant, but it is also imperceptible due to the blind-spot incorporated into our perception at an early stage by the living language.

This symbiosis has had a profound effect on the actual physiological development of the brain, not only in the recent evolution of the brain, but also in the re-organization of localized synaptic relations during the early life of the human. This cerebral manifestation of the living language is detailed in the following section.

The House of the Living Language

At birth the brain is largely committed as to function; the occipital lobe is programmed for vision, the motor cortex can already direct purposeful movement, and yet there is another part of the brain that is largely *uncommitted* at birth[11], an area with no programming. This area includes the future speech centres, located in the left (generally dominant) hemisphere, and the future interpretive cortex, which is located on the dorsal surfaces of the temporal lobes on both sides of the brain. (Figure 4) Obviously then, specific languages are not an implicit activity of the human brain. Evolution has given us a sizable portion of grey matter earmarked for language imprinting: the speech centres which can be programmed for very diverse languages; however, the language imprinted is an autonomous system (ontogenically speaking).

As the two-year-old begins to trace and imprint the engrams of English, a magical activity takes place within the child's brain. In a slow dance as beautiful and complex as meiosis, changes occur in the microstructure of synapses[12]. Synaptic buds form and neurotransmitters invade new areas & trigger their first series of ionic discharges. The living language slowly but surely invades the brain of the young human and arranges its House with sure and precise hands.

The interpretive cortex, the other area 'uncommitted' at birth, is devoted to the interpretation of present experience in the light of past experience. It is also proximal to the speech centres. As it assumes its function of analyzing experience and establishing the individual's place in the world, the interpretive cortex is modified by the speech centre, to which it refers for concept materialization. In this manner, the strong and alien circuitry of the speech centre floods into the interpretive cortex during its formative development and mutates its circuitry. This is the beach-head of the Governor. The section of the brain which presents reality to consciousness is insidiously distorted. This process creates a decisive dichotomy of brain and mind which in turn becomes a major 'stumbling block' in the path of total hemispheric consciousness (nirvana), where the brain and body are permeated by mind.

The functional necessities of the living language (in this case English) codify the internal circuitry of the interpretive cortex in both hemispheres via the corpus callosum (the connection between the two hemispheres). The modified interpretive cortex and speech centre together make up the House of the living language.

The parasitization of experience by the living language is, as we have seen, facilitated by the House of the living language. However, the specialized tissue which delineates the House of the living language is not isolated to the degree that it attains in the special case represented by the poet. Here, the demands on the specialized tissue result in a truly radical departure from holistic brain function *and* a release from the parasitization of experience (third depersonalization). In a brain junta whose generals are the neurotransmitters, the House of the living language takes the final step and becomes the Parasite.

(The specialized demands placed on the House of the living language by the writer's mind place the Parasite slightly outside the normal control mechanisms of both the living language and the mind, but, because the parasite is subject to will, it tends to affiliate itself with mind.)

The Parasite

The manner in which the House of the living language evolves into the Parasite hinges on neurotransmitters & axonal / dendritic growth. The following is a brief illustrated survey of neuronal / brain function in order to clarify this process.

FIGURE 2: Two Neurones with Expanded View of Synapse

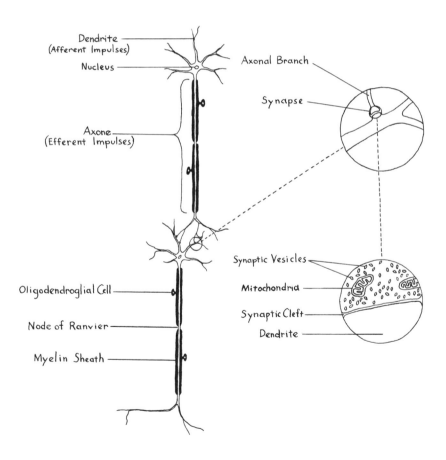

Figure 2 illustrates two columnar neurones from the cortex with an expansion of the synaptic cleft. In the brain, grey matter corresponds to a concentration of neuronal nucleii, white matter corresponds to concentrations of neuronal axones[6]. The dendrites of the neurone receive afferent (incoming) impulses and the neurone is either excited or inhibited by this impulse. If excited the cell 'fires' and an impulse is generated which travels along the axone (the efferent impulse) until it reaches the nerve ending of the axone. It is then transmitted across the synaptic cleft by a specific neurotransmitter.

Neurotransmitters are present in the extra-neuronal (glial) space and in the vesicles which can be seen in the third enlargement of the diagram. The vesicles release transmitters, the mitochondria metabolize (neutralize) them. The major neurotransmitters of the brain are the amines; Acetycholine, Dopamine, Norpinephrine, Serotonin (which incidentally has the greatest concentration of cell bodies just under Penfield's location for the 'seat of mind' in the diencephalon, see Figure 5) and Histamine.[7] These transmitters, generally referred to as the *monoamines,* are affected by a wide variety of pharmacological agents. *Dale's Law* holds that 'each neurone uses only one transmitter in its informational transactions' however, several transmitters may be present in localized regions of the brain.

An impulse, after reaching the target cell can also be translated into an *intracellular* response. This is effected by a neurochemical called Cyclic adenosine $3':5'$ — monophosphate (cAMP). cAMP levels are highest in the brain. cAMP mediates the effects of hormones on their target cells, also, cAMP synthesis is *increased* by both electrical stimulation and neurotransmitter presence. In fact, cAMP is very important because in response to increased levels of certain neurotransmitters (which themselves are the mediators of the mind's will, due to the close proximity of most transmitter axonal-tracts and pathways to the mind in the diencephalon) cAMP can effect *structural changes* (plastic changes) in the neurones, enlarging them & increasing their potency. Also, by increasing dendritic & synaptic connections, cAMP mediates *co-cellular* 'cascade' reactions [9]. Thus, sustained firing of specific neurones or groups of neurones effects major neurochemical & neuroelectrical changes of these clusters, as well as plastic changes in the physiology of the cells through the cascade reaction. Figure 3, a schematic diagram of Synapse & Monoamine/ CAMP functions, illustrates basic synaptic chemistry.

FIGURE 3: Schematic Diagram of Synapse & Monoamine/ CAMP Functions with Actions of Psychoactive Chemicals

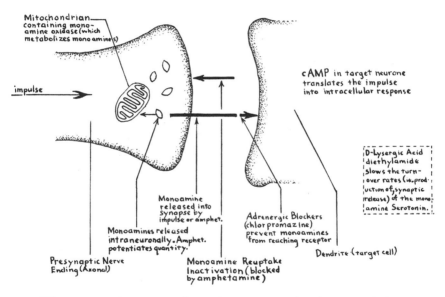

The neurone is connected to other neurones by the synaptic junctions. The brain represents 10^{11} neurones interconnected in an unimaginable static choreography of sub-systems and interchanges not simplified by the fact that each neurone can have a thousand or more synaptic junctions on its surface. The sum of this complex structure is represented by the cerebral cortex, illustrated in Figure 4. The smaller diagram accompanying this illustration gives a rough location of the parasite. I will now describe the development & function of the parasite.

FIGURE 4: The Cerebral Cortex·
Dominant Hemisphere

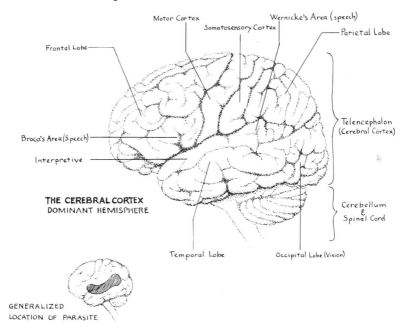

Entropy in the brain is manifested by the basal tendency of thought towards habitual patterning. In brain-trauma, psychotic states & obsessive behaviour (such as 'punding' where an amphetamine psychosis precipitates repetitive movements or gestures), thought becomes stereotyped & exhibits perseverance & reduplication. The instinctual brain, characterized by its tendency towards habituation, passively resists creative human intelligence, which is seized like chaos from the heart of order.

In this one crucial area the House of the living language does *not* escape the basal tendency of the brain. In fact, grammar is as inviolate in sleep-talkers as it is in fully conscious humans. Therefore, even though the House of the living language differs substantially from the rest of the brain it is not nearly as radically distinct as the Parasite, which subsumes the House in the case of the poet.

The writer, particularly the poet, places an unusual demand on the speech centre, and this demand is for *novel configurations*. Novel configuration is not to be confused with 'novelty for the sake of'. All writers resist the feedback tendencies of perseverance in phrasing, if not recurrent words. Thus, the writer, and most particularly the poet, requires novel configurations in order to create a forward motion idealized by its transcendence over unconscious entropy. The poet cultivates a sort of voluntary paraphasia[10], and it is *this* functional overriding of the House of the living language that reorganizes the neurochemistry & cascade reactions of the House into the cryptic & capricious circuitry of the Parasite. The Parasite is designated as such because its chemistry & function differ so radically from the rest of the brain. It becomes the most localized of localizations, yet, it draws its sustenance, in the form of information & purpose, from the brain and mind respectively. A true Parasite, it also impinges on consciousness. (This will be dealt with below.)

Because the Muses are the daughters of memory it seems reasonable to assume that the neurotransmitters whose altered levels determine the boundary of the Parasite would also be memory specific, ie; with axonal tracts & pathways connected to the hippocampus, a structure integral to both the storing and retrieval of memory in the brain (Figure 5). These neurotransmitters are Norepinephrine and Acetycholine. I include Serotonin with these also, not because it is memory specific, but because of its association with consciousness and mind. The altered levels of norepinephrine, acetycholine and serotonin in the formative Parasite, mediated by elevated levels of cAMP, give rise to cascade reactions which in turn re-figure the House of the living language.

Now, we return to the effects of the Parasite on the consciousness of the poet. Obviously such a major neuronal re-organization must have an effect on consciousness, as the brain normally functions fairly holistically (despite the House). And it does have an effect, the literature is fraught with references to it; Rimbaud's '*dérèglement de tous les sens*', Keat's 'negative capability' etc. However, like a nuclear reactor which generates novel configurations instead of power, the parasite is maintained like a kind of schizophrenic fission by the control-rods of the mind. These control-rods, which maintain the Parasite at the subcritical level, consist of the religious/ philosophical posture assumed by the mind to prevent this and other 'critical' reactions within the brain, though (and history bears this out) not always successfully.

The Parasite also bestows a peculiar side effect, a fringe benefit if you like, on the mind. It releases the conceptual hold of the Governor slightly and allows the mind to fuel the Parasite itself into the realm of nirvana, though the mind does not follow it (there have been exceptions). It is this process which makes a Galahad out of the poet, able to reveal the Grail to others, but not to himself.

The Parasite allows the poet to function beyond his own capability.

In the hypernormal cogitation of the Parasite, thought processes & conceptualizations assemble themselves at inhuman speed & on awesome scales. The artificial energy derived from controlled neurochemical 'schizophrenia' drives the Parasite far beyond the perceptions of its host.

FIGURE 5: The Brain Stem

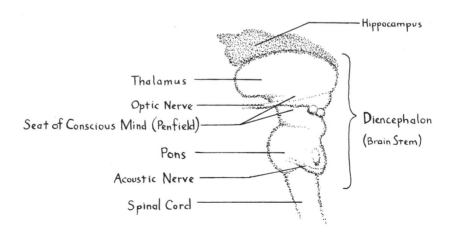

References

1. Jacques Monod, *Chance & Necessity,* Random House, 1971.
2. Jack Spicer, *Vancouver Lectures,* 1965.
3. Hubert Benoît, *Let Go,* Samuel Weiser, 1973.
4. Benjamin Lee Whorf, *Language Thought & Reality,* M.I.T. Press, 1956.
5. William S. Burroughs, *Exterminator,* Viking Compass, 1966.
6. Keith Oatley, *Brain Mechanisms and Mind,* Thames & Hudson, 1972.
7. Solomon H. Snyder, *Catecholamines, Serotonin, & Histamine,* Little Brown & Company, *Basic Neurochemistry,* 1976.
8. Richard Hammerschlag & Eugene Roberts, *Overview of Chemical Transmission,* Little, Brown & Company, *Basic Neurochemistry,* 1976.
9. James A. Nathanson & Paul Greengard, *Cyclic Nucleotides and Synaptic Transmission,* Little, Brown & Company, *Basic Neurochemistry,* 1976.
10. Bernard Goddery, *Three Models of Brain Function and their Implications for the Treatment of Aphasic Patients,* M.A. Thesis, University of Waterloo, 1977.
11. Wilder Penfield, *The Mystery of the Mind,* Princeton, 1975.
12. John C. Eccles, *The Understanding of the Brain,* McGraw Hill, 1977.

The Dialectic Criminal

Colloquial phrases composed of words whose literal meaning is other than the context in which they are used I call *dialectic metaphors*. These units can almost be regarded as single words. They have been constructed by the communal mind to solve morphemic problems inherent in English & surmountable only by using these phrases.

There are two distinct classes to these infra-dialectical metaphors. One class is an outmoded historical connotation, ie 'Put your nose to the grindstone.' while the other class is a purely abstract or nominative procedure giving us 'Head in the clouds.' at its most metaphorical and 'Hairy man, hairy.' or 'Come on.' at its most abstract. It is this latter category which comprises most of the following story.

Hand in Glove with an Old Hat

When it's raining cats and dogs you've got to cut corners because you could get your eyes peeled. You must come to grips with yourself until you fly off the handle & then if you're not fit as a fiddle you'll spill the beans. That's hitting below the belt with the short end of the stick, if I can bring the point home ladies.

*

It all started in early 1975, I had an axe to grind during a blanket freeze. It was no great shakes but I had to go against the grain, iron out the details. You see, I pulled a few strings & had to go off the deep end. But I guess I had reckoned without my host. (That's burning the candle at both ends because this whole thing rings a bell.) The host carried a torch for this chick & now she's praying through the nose. I guess the handwriting was on the wall though.

Anyway, before I got the drop on this I bit the dust and turned the tables. I caught the big shot hanging around by a thread generally laying it on the line. I told him I thought he was right off the wall and it went to his head. He kept it under his hat but greased my palms anyway. Yet I always say strike while the iron is hot and lay low till the heat's off because drawing a line is like splitting hairs. I'd be in the groove now if it wasn't for a bolt out of the blue & even then I got taken to the cleaners. But the whole kit and caboodle is right as rain by my money.

You on the other hand, you put your foot in your mouth & bit off more than you could chew. Now with what's left you put your foot in the door and then accuse *me* of changing my tune? I *had* to change my tune in order to face the music.

I'm going through the motions after bringing the house down because a fly-by-night that held water led me down the garden path. I'm coming on like this because I put one over on you. And now you're out on a limb getting a charge. If you hadn't swapped horses in midstream maybe you could've gotten off. But you've got to keep the ball rolling because you're playing with loaded dice. But then again, who am I to remain on the level?

Anyway back in '75 I was riding a dark horse with a grain of salt up my sleeve. I burned my bridges as I got to them. Everyone around me was starting from scratch because they threw in their towels. I was going like a bat out of hell, I got the drop on it under my skin. A drop in the bucket that is, so now I'm right down your alley because I blew my top. 'In hot water?' you ask, no, just flashing. I'm making tracks because this place is definitely nothing by mouth, by word of mouth that is. You see, when you're over your head in a car pool & no one is biting then it's time to break the ice. And break the ice I did, lemme tell you, this bruiser I double crossed was loaded for bear. I figured it was time to throw a monkey wrench into the works when suddenly he pulled a boner. I didn't waste any time, I hit him below the belt and buried the hatchet. It's a dog's breakfast, lemme tell you, when you're hand in glove with an old hat.

Now I'm letting it all hang out in my old stomping grounds and you can go and take the cake because I've been beating around the burning bush long enough. I've got a stiff upper lip from blowing hot and cold on you bad eggs. I'll never let by-gones become old stand-bys because the leading edge takes the friction.

You're shitting bricks but I'm sweating blood.

Homographs and the Discharge of Connotation in the Poem

The outstanding attribute of words in a poem is their transcendence of taxonomy. All the levels of meaning inherent in one line can only be realized by the poly-connotative recombinant interpretation of fixed terms arising out of the basal lexicon.

Poly-connotation builds up a static charge within the poem. Because the resting potential of this static charge is at an elevated level in relation to standard language use it discharges easily. (In the improvisational poetry of the last few decades it seemed that this precise attribute was the final irreducible core, the most characteristic quality of the poem.) The elevated charge consequently alters the lexemic status of the words in the poem. They become homographs (heteronyms), host to a halo of meanings, much like the masts of (a ship) at sea crowned by St. Elmo's fire. (This deck is rigged.)

Hypothetically, the fabrication of a poem composed almost entirely of 'real' homographs taken from the lexicon would demonstrate the propensities of the connotative charge. The refinement, distillation & compacting of these 'heavy metals' of the lexicon should bring about a fusion reaction, entailing the release of enough energy to shed light on both connotation & 'ambiguity'.

I found approx. 175 homographs in the OED, though only 165 of these I found suitable (simply out of preference for terms, ie I found one of the meanings banal). Of this number it seemed only about 50 could be syntactically joined in a meaningful sequence.

The following construct is the result of this research.

My Point an Order
My point an order
in the drift of states.
Sounds steep in the rush above the bow &
O the feeling winds!
To utter light & direct tender,
as a bluff articulates the decline
of our quarry.
Scale matter stemmed the rings.
The stroke conducted a current right
to the ground bolting.
A model brush drew the charge,
sought console of the rest.
Possibly a host of palms
or the pole
we tend to.
Not stalked or cast by lines baited.
                              Content being
where the tear lies.

It is interesting to note the mathematics involved in the use of 'in situ' homographs. One homograph can have two to five meanings. General usage only implies two, though taxonomically there may be more.

Each homograph alters the meaning of the sentence containing it as many times as there are interpretations of the homograph. The meaning multiplies by a factor of 2 (general usage) with each successive homograph in the sentence, ie 2 homographs = 4 meanings (interpretations) of the text. The equation for interpretive combinations of homographs in a sentence is X to the power of y, where X = the meanings of each homograph and y the number of homographs in the sentence.

The final connotative discharge (the transfer of meaning from text to perceiver), is invariant, though the minor connotations can be as variable as the number of perceivers. The discharge is a revelation, the simultaneous illumination of the sum recombinant connotations. In structure this process is analogous to a dendritic tree, or lightning, the branches being all the tributaries of meaning upstream from the final discharge. This is what is meant when one says 'the Poem always seeks the shortest distance between two points'.

Typeset in Bembo and printed in Canada
in an edition of 1000 copies, at
The Coach House Press,
401 (rear) Huron Street,
Toronto, Canada M5S 2G5